Handwriting by George

Rules of Civility & Decent Behavior

To Draw & Write
In Company and conversation
Rules 56-83

Greenleaf Press,
Lebanon , TN

Thanks:
To the wonderful "Tall" Sarah our daughter(in-law) and Jon, our much loved and oldest experimental model, for taking this idea and making it happen!

published by Greenleaf Books, LLC

Internet: www.greenleafpress.com
3761 Highway 109 N., Unit D
Lebanon, TN 37087
615-449-1617

Greenleaf Press

For further information visit our website at www.GreenleafPress.com

Introduction
and notes for parents & teachers

When George Washington was sixteen years old, he began copying 110 maxims for polite behavior into his schoolbooks. These rules describe the behavior of a gentleman, and many claim that they greatly influenced Washington's attitudes and standards for his own behavior.

Several years ago we became aware of George Washington's ***Rule's of Decency and Civility****. We were all tired of the standard handwriting practice book copy material and began using Washington's* ***Rules*** *as copy work. While many of them have obvious application to the eighteenth century, they also have a lot to say to modern gentlemen and ladies. We hadn't expected to enjoy these sayings as much as we did. They rarely stayed merely copywork exercise but became the basis of other discussions. "Show nothing to your friend that might affright him," became a part of a discussion about why the children should not torment our guests (particularly the one with the intense mouse phobia) ith the dead mouse discovered under the sink. Other rules addressed issues involving putting others first and self last - and other ways to show respect to those around us.*

In this book, we have included rules 56-83, with another volume to follow that will complete the set. For each rule, there is space to copy it at least once, and space to draw an illustration for each one. Be sure to talk about the ways you can apply the rule to your relationships with those around you. Enjoy!

Cyndy Shearer

Rule 56

Associate yourself with Men of good Quality if you Esteem your own Reputation; for 'tis better to be alone than in bad Company.

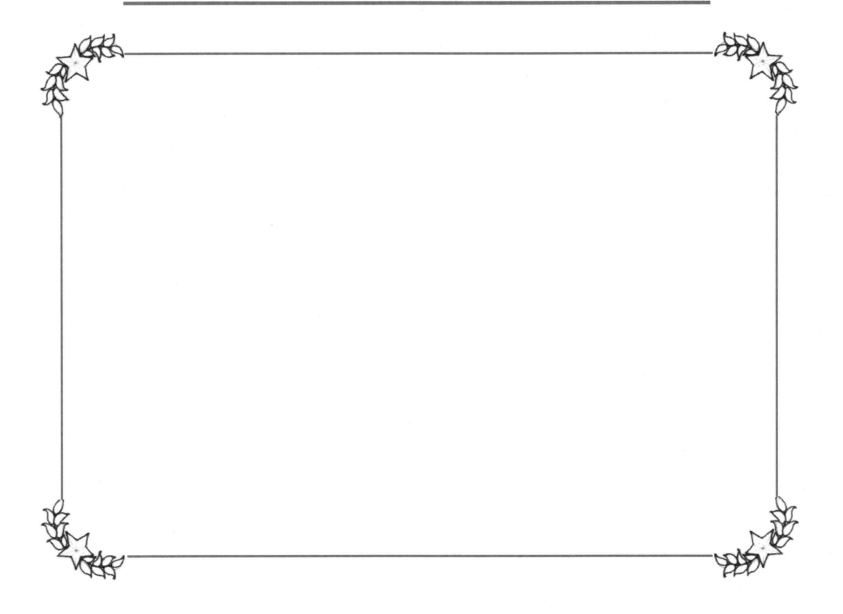

Rule 57a

In walking with One Greater than yourself, let him walk on the Right and Stop not till he does and be not the first that turns, and when you do turn let it be with your face towards him.

Rule 57b

In walking with a Man of Great Quality, walk not with him Cheek by Jowl but Somewhat behind him; but yet in Such a Manner that he may easily Speak to you.

Rule 58

Let your Conversation be without Malice or Envy, for 'tis a Sign of a Tractable and Commendable Nature. And in all Causes of Passion admit Reason to Govern.

Rule 59

Never express anything unbecoming, nor Act against the Rules Moral before your inferiors.

Rule 60

Be not immodest in urging your Friends to Discover a Secret.

Rule 61

Utter not base and frivolous things amongst grave and Learned Men nor very Difficult Questions or Subjects among the Ignorant, or things hard to be believed, Stuff not your Discourse with Sentences amongst your Betters nor Equals.

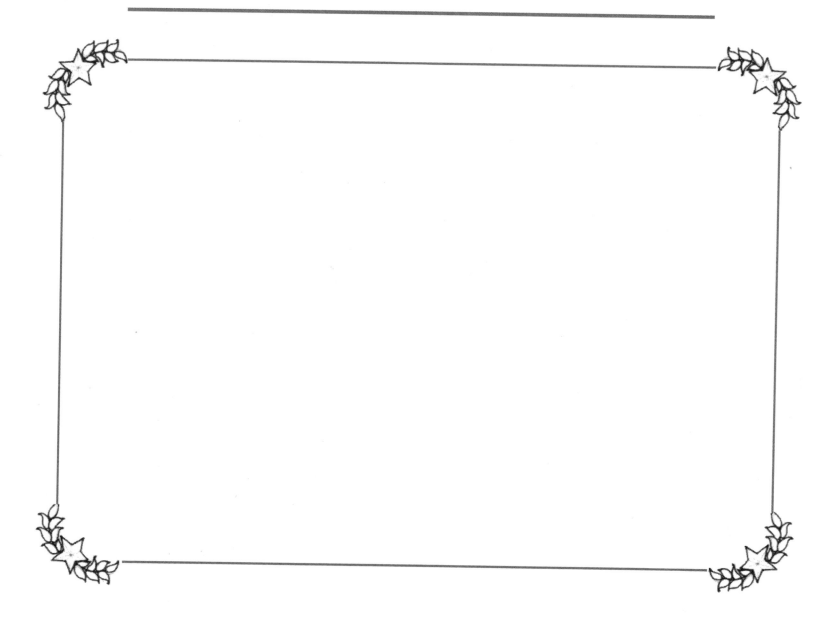

Rule 62

Speak not of doleful Things in a Time of Mirth or at the Table. Speak not of Melancholy Things as Death and Wounds, and if others Mention them Change if you can the Discourse. Tell not your Dreams, but to your intimate Friend.

Rule 63

A Man ought not to value himself of his Achievements, or rare Qualities of Wit; much less of his Riches, Virtue, or Kindred.

Rule 64

Break not a Jest where none take pleasure in mirth
Laugh not aloud, nor at all without Occasion, deride no man's
Misfortune, though there Seem to be Some cause.

Rule 65

Speak not injurious Words neither in Jest nor Earnest. Scoff at none although they give Occasion.

Rule 66

Be not froward but friendly and Courteous; the first to Salute, hear, and answer. Be not Pensive when it is a time to Converse.

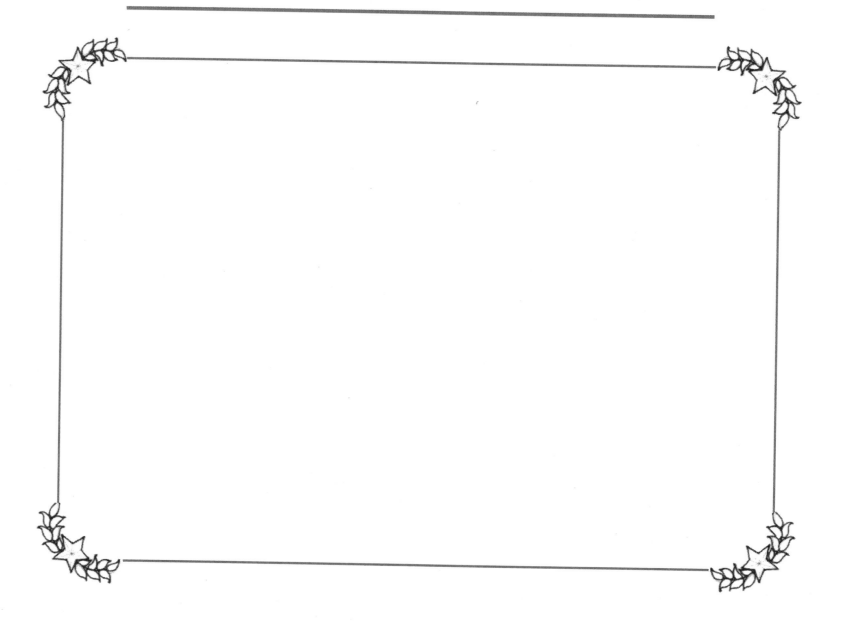

Rule 67

Detract not from others, neither be excessive in Commanding.

Rule 68

Go not thither, where you know not, whether you Shall be Welcome or not. Give not Advice without being Asked & when desired do it briefly.

Rule 69

If two contend together take not the part of either unconstrained; and be not obstinate in your own Opinion, in Things indifferent be of the Major Side.

Rule 70

Reprehend not the imperfections of others for that belongs to Parents, Masters, and Superiors.

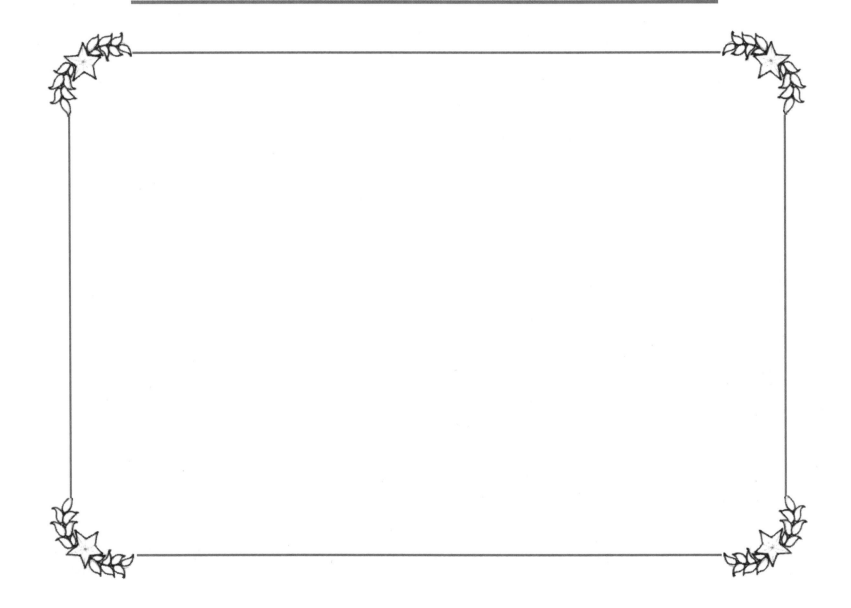

Rule 71

Gaze not on the marks or blemishes of Others and ask not how they came. What you may Speak in Secret to your Friend deliver not before others.

Rule 72

Speak not in an unknown Tongue in Company but in
your own Language and that as those of Quality do and not
as the Vulgar; Sublime matters treat Seriously.

Rule 73

Think before you Speak. Pronounce not imperfectly nor bring out your Words too hastily but orderly & distinctly.

Rule 74

When Another Speaks be attentive your Self and disturb not the Audience. If any hesitate in his Words help him not nor Prompt him unless desired. Interrupt him not, nor Answer him till his Speech be ended.

Rule 75

In the midst of Discourse, ask not of what one treateth but if you Perceive any Stop because of your coming you may well intreat him gently to Proceed. If a Person of Quality comes in while you are Conversing it's handsome to Repeat what was said before.

Rule 76

While you are talking, Point not with your Finger at him of Whom you Discourse nor Approach too near him to whom you talk, especially to his face.

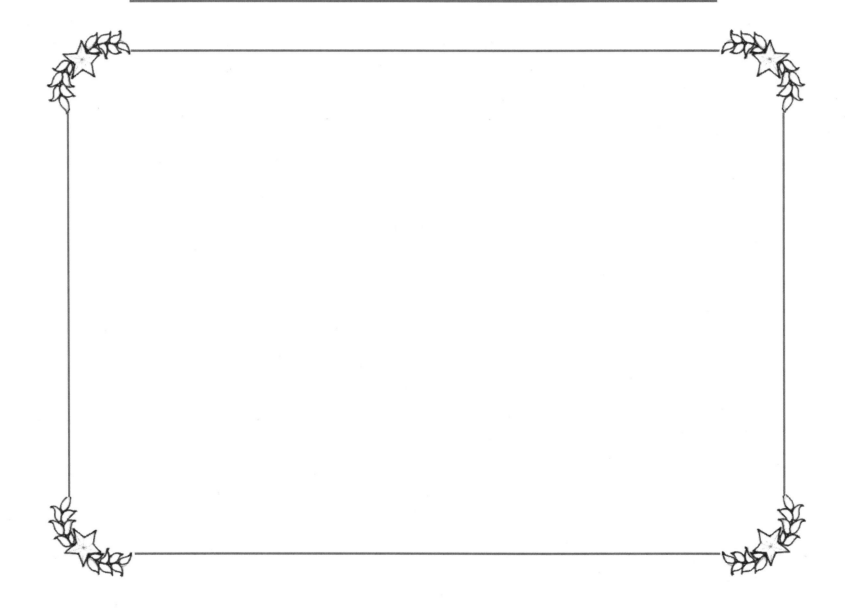

Rule 77

Treat with men at fit Times about Business & Whisper not in the Company of Others.

Rule 78

Make no Comparisons and if any of the Company be Commended for any brave act of Virtue, commend not another for the Same.

Rule 79

Be not apt to relate News if you know not the truth thereof. In Discoursing of things you Have heard, Name not your Author always. A Secret Discover not.

Rule 80

Be not Tedious in Discourse or in reading unless you find the Company pleased therewith.

Rule 81

Be not Curious to Know the Affairs of Others neither approach those that Speak in Private.

Rule 82

Undertake not what you cannot Perform, but be Careful to keep your Promise.

Rule 83

When you deliver a matter, do it without Passion & with Discretion, however mean the Person be you do it to.

5514866R0

Made in the USA
Charleston, SC
25 June 2010